Rich black people.

Introduction.

This book is not a theory book; it is entirely practical and goes to the root of why many black people or descendants of Africans fail to find happiness and wealth. The text is straight and clear; if the reader memorizes this book, he won't have to go looking for similar books.

In this book, you will find the most important points after reading dozens of books about classical African and European philosophy, spirituality, history, personal development, economics and finance. All this combined with my own life experience.

This book has few pages, but I would have summarized all in a single sentence:

"In life, we are what we think most of the day"

But what are you thinking about? Are you aware of your thoughts? Why are you thinking what you think? There are many questions, but let's start with this:

Why is Africa poor?

The only reason that Africa is poor is because the television says that, there is no other reason. Also the Africans think that they are poor because they watch too much television, and they accept all the negative publicity and negative images that are sent to them.

Africa is the richest continent on the planet; everyone goes there to seek its oil, its diamonds, its minerals, its wood, its large reserves of water, to fish in its waters, to enjoy its wildlife and other countless riches.

So, why do Africans and everyone says that Africa is poor?

Because some people want Africans to feel and THINK that they are poor, incapable and useless, so that others can take their wealth, there is no other reason.

The solution to a poor Africa or poor black people is a change in their THINKING, a way of negative THINKING that they have been taught for hundreds of years with the sole intention of keeping them domesticated.

European historians and thinkers first worked to justify slavery, and then colonialism. Changed the ancient African history and sent negative messages about blank men and women to everyone, with the sole purpose of making believe that Africans have never done anything important, even in their own land, and thus maintain the so-called "white supremacy."

All this is history, and although I am aware that the negative publicity against black men and women around the world continues today, the solution to the poor and unhappy MENTALITY is very simple, and is explained in this book.

In this book, I have written a bit about the history of Africa, but it is imperative that anyone with African roots studies the African history, that goes further than slavery and thinks about the great future that they can have, especially the African men and women that live in Africa, this wonderful continent full with all the riches the world wants.

The African history was changed and all ancient black civilizations traces were erased. The Sudanese, Ethiopians and later the Egyptians created the greatest civilizations, invented science, arts and religion. The more important mystics were also imported from Africa.

The Greeks learned from black people and created their own civilization, somehow more materialistic than the African civilizations. The "Greek miracle" does not exist, through history everyone has learned from someone and only Black people were the first.

Why have they hidden all the positive evidences about the Black people? Why has there been so much publicity given to Greece and "blanked history"?

Why have they blocked or falsified the contribution of Black people to the universal civilization?

One of the main reasons was to justify slavery, the other to maintain the so-called "white supremacy".

But as I said, all this is history. Black, white, yellow, brown, all are children of the Creation and, all have a God that is within each one:

"The kingdom of God is within you" - Luke 17:21

We all have the same brain, the same legs, the same arms, the same will and the same ability to improve our attitude. None was created different by God.

"God created mankind in his own image, in the image of God he created them;" - Genesis 1:26-27

For the black men and women to be rich and happy, they simply have to erase or delete what they have been taught for hundreds of years, and change their mindset.

This book will explain how to do it, and if you follow each step and are consistent, it will be no reason why you cannot achieve your goals. Remember that you are made in the image and likeness of God, and God within you.

Chapter 1. Who is the Black?

The Black is the firstborn of creation, son of earth, born in Africa and from him born the Egyptian, Arabic and Atlantes.

The Black was the most numerous and dominated the earth for thousands of years. Sudanese, Ethiopians and Egyptians later, created the greatest civilizations, invented the science, the arts and religion, were also the most important mystics.

The Greeks learned from black people and created their own civilization, something more materialistic than the Africans. The "Greek miracle" does not exist, throughout history everyone has learned from someone and, only the Black people were the first.

The Black created the Egyptian and Ethiopia civilizations, The Ife and Benin civilizations, the Lake Chad civilizations, the Ghana and the so called Neo-Sudanese civilizations.

Black people lived all around the continent, including Egypt, but they were mixed with primitive nomad conquerors and Asian traders, all white foreigners.

In recent centuries of Ancient Egypt, the Nile Delta was full of foreign whites: Copts, Persians, Trojans, Carians and Ionians. This is the only reason why today the North of Africa is "clearer" than the south. Even today, African features clearly continue in the habitants of North Africa and parts of southern Europe.

Egypt was conquered by the Persians in 525 BC, then by Alexander, by the Romans in 50 BC, by the Arabs in the seventh century, the Turks in the sixteenth century, by Napoleon and finally by English in the late eighteenth century.

Across the Nile valley were several civilizations with over 10,000 years old while the world was barbarian and, although they were destroyed by many invasions, Black people remained being the light for many young people from the Mediterranean, who came to learn its ancient scientists, mystics, religious and moral knowledge.

From the fifteenth century, the Portuguese, Dutch, English, French, Danes, Germans and Spaniards began to trade with the Atlantic African coast, European seafarers fond that African states were equivalent or better than European states, although technological development was lower.

The Black invented the iron, but not the guns, also used gunpowder, but not for war.

The first navigators who reached the African Atlantic coast discovered the Africans had well equipped roads, decorated with trees, men and women were dressed nicely on the streets.

Upon arrival to the Kingdom of Congo, they saw well-dressed people in silks and fine fabrics, well organized states with large sovereign and developed industry.

Mozambique also had a well-formed state, comparable to the Europe of the fifteenth century civilization.

But Europeans were hungry for slaves, and to justify the slave trade, they said that the black men and women were semi-animals, a commodity.

This European invention destroyed all civilizations in Africa, and filled the Black people with complex, which still lasts today.

When Christopher Columbus discovered America, slaves were required to exploit the new lands, and the Black people became the new workforce.

In the Middle Ages, slavery was normal in Europe and Africa, even many African emperors had white slaves, but these slaves lived with families, and it was more like people who served in a home for few years.

In Africa, it was unthinkable that a slave was treated as an object, and for some African ethnic groups such as the Fangs, the slavery did not exist.

The European slave trade was totally unknown; it became an economic need and a very lucrative business. Black slave was treated as a commodity, and thanks to its technology Europeans began to belittle the African world.

The memory of Black civilizations that spread around the world was almost forgotten. Today, this memory lives on many ruins and libraries along Africa. One of the clearest memories is the Sphinx, Pharaoh's image, with black head. But you can find thousands of evidence throughout the Nile Valley, from the Great Lakes to the Delta and Sudan.

The Black people extended throughout the Mediterranean populations, and whites were economic and culturally inferior. Greek, Asia Minor, the Etruscans in Italy, the Gauls that worshiped Black Virgins, Paris means "Temple of Isis" or "For Isis".

The British were blacks who got there crossing France. A black king named Gormund ruled Ireland. Even some Germanic people worshiped Isis, the Black.

Many Western scholars and historians know all this and more, but we the Africans and African descendants are the ones who have to rewrite our history for our good.

African colonization destroyed cultural ties, and there originated dialects and forced the Africans to fight or hide in the jungle for centuries, they abandoned their land, possessions and forgetting all its history.

The Black people were forced to live in hiding, like animals in the jungle.

Africans became increasingly vile and adapted to the forest, for this reason, in the documentaries recorded by white and promoted worldwide, the African are seen living like wilds.

We all know that Black people´s history in the last 500 years is full of killings, looting, exploitation, misery and oppression, but all this has finished, now everything is different and the future can be changed.

I wrote this book for every black man and women that is thinking about what´s their priority, what are their principles and help them to achieve their goals.

Black, white, yellow or brown, all should live with a goal in mind, the opportunities are equal for all, we all have the same power, same arms, same legs, same heart, the same brain, the same will and the same ability to THINK and IMAGINE.

There is nothing that the men and women cannot IMAGINE and DO with faith and trust in God, which is within us.

"If you can believe, all things are possible to him who believes." - Mark 9:23

The enemy is not the White nor west, neither banks nor the multinational, or the Illuminati, the greatest enemy of man is the fear and doubt in God, the God that is within all of us.

The negative publicity towards the Black people has made them believe that they are unworthy, but that's a lie, know your history and contribute to the further growth of yourselves and your family.

Europe and the West are ruined, the only reason they are still rich is because they believe that they are.

Africans live in the world's richest continent, but are poor because in their mind they THINK they are poor.

You only have to change your mindset, stop thinking that you are poor and that someone else has to come to help you. The wealth and happiness of any man or woman is only assured if they get it for themselves.

We black men and women have been suffering due to television advertising that destroys our hopes, our ambitions and the confidence in us.

Before television, tons of literature was printed to convince the Blacks and Africans that in Africa there were only wilds, and Africa is full of cannibals, where no civilized being should go, but everyone is going to this continent to seek its wealth.

You have to love Africa; you have to love your origins. To become rich and happy it is absolutely essential to be proud of our race, if you do not love and respect ourselves, you cannot love and respect God that is within you.

We've all have seen African migrants who say that they are Americans, because they are ashamed of their origin, I also know black Americans or Europeans who do not want to be reminded about their African origin, as if they could hide it…

In order to become rich and happy, you have to be proud of whom you are and where you came from, it is essential. God made you well and, you have to give thanks every day.

Although the negative publicity against the Black people is fully and actuality implemented, it is no longer an excuse, every man or woman, Black, White, Yellow or
Brown is able to improve his character, dominate
his will, direct his life and meet his goals. God put the man

and women on earth as his creation, every man or women that live on fear or doubt is insulting the God that is within him.

If someone is poor and unhappy, he must ask himself about what he or she is THINGKING about most of the time, which IMAGE of himself he or she has in his mind, do you see a lazy person without will?

If you want to be happy and rich, change the image you have of yourself, IMAGINE yourself with confidence, sure about getting your goals, active and happy in all you do.

It's time to not blame anyone for your mistakes, it's time to take responsibility, it's time to not give up, not to depend on other to do for you what you should do for yourself, it's time to trust the God that is within you, to have faith that you will make it.

"Truly I tell you, if you have faith as small as a mustard seed, nothing will be impossible for you." - Matthew 17:20

Slavery did a lot of damage, but there is no longer any reason for this damage to continue lasting.

Chapter 2. Why be rich and happy?

Every man and woman has the right to be free and develop mentally, spiritually and physically. Every man and woman has the right to surround themselves with elegance, beauty and wealth, asking for less than you want is a mistake.

To be happy a man or woman must have love, and there is nothing that makes anyone happier than give, no matter if they are Black, White, Yellow or Brown. The man or woman who has nothing to give to their husband, wife, father, children, community, etc, cannot be happy.

If you want to be rich and happy it is possible, it does not depend on where you live. If you live in the jungle, you are surrounded by wealth, the only reason that you may be poor is because you THINK like a poor person; there is no other reason for you to be poor.

If you do not find the love of your life, it is because you do not THINK you can get it, if you really believe that you can get it, you would. It is not because you THINK you're ugly, fat or short, we all have seen these kinds of people with the love of their lives.

All depends on what you THINK you can get.

"And whatever you ask in prayer, you will receive, if you have faith." - Matthew 21:22

To get what you want, you do not have to be extremely talented, we all know rich people that have not a special talent married with beauties. Their only talent is that they THINK that deserve the best.

Many intelligent people with good careers are poor or in debt, many beautiful people are single, many people who were born rich are poor, all the new rich families come from poor or middle class families.

It doesn´t matter if you are the poorest man or woman, or if you are in debt, it doesn´t matter if you do not have important friends or other kind of resources to get started. What matters is what you THINK you are, THINK that you are rich, healthy and happy, or whatever you want, and you will be.

What matters is what you THINK and the FAITH you have about getting what you want.

But to THINK about what you want is not enough if you do not put some ACTION, putting some ACTION towards what you want is as important as maintaining a mental image with FAITH and GRATITUDE for what you want. You cannot achieve anything without ACTION, the ACTION is as important as your THOUGHTS.

You may not want to be rich; you might just want to be happy. But what is happiness? For each person happiness is different, for some happiness is to have a partner, others want to be cured of a disease, end a career or have a new car.

For me happiness is to enjoy every day, THANKS God that is within me for giving me the opportunity to be in this world.

But if you want to get something, first you have to know what you want, you have to be very sure of what you want and not change every so often.

"When you ask, you must believe and not doubt, because the one who doubts is like a wave of the sea, blown and tossed by the wind. 7 That person should not expect to receive anything from the Lord. 8 Such a person is double-minded and unstable in all they do". - James 1:6-8

Once you know what you want, IMAGINE enjoying that thing or the qualities you want to have, keep this picture in your mind and be happy, like you had already got it, feel it, and be grateful to God that is within you for giving it to you.

Have FAITH and never doubt. This is a prayer.

Chapter 3. Will to take action, be thankful and love.

When you know what you really want and, you have happily imagined that you already have it, take ACTION.

You have to take ACTION every day with FAITH and a mental picture of what you want. Do all you can do each day, THINK that the most important is not to do many things, but most important is that what you do, you do it well.

If what you do each day, you do it well, even a little, at end of the day you will be happier, and if every day you are happier, your life will be happier and richer.

You do not have to do things you do not like, but at times you may, for some time, have to do something you do not like to get what you want.

Never doubt, keep your vision and enjoy it while giving thanks for having achieved what you want, keep your FAITH about getting your goal.

If things do not work out at the beginning, do not worry, every fight and every defeat will make you smarter and stronger, braver, more skilled and more confident.

The problems are not problems, if you have FAITH in what you are IMAGINING is coming, you will be better every day. You cannot lose if you have FAITH in God that is within you.

If you have good habits you'll be happy and rich, but you already know it. There is no need to say that drinking too much, eating too much, smoking too much and watching too much television will not help you on the path to wealth and happiness.

Having a clear goals and focus on them, plus reading many books, are two of the best habits you can have.

Daily reading and learning from books that others have written, it is a price you pay to be happy and rich. Why not take advantage of the experience of other rich and happy people? You can learn from your own experience, but if you learn from your role model, it will be much easier.

THANK God every day, give thanks for dawn each day, give thanks to the rain, give thanks for being born, give thanks during the night. Give thanks every moment that you're happy, but also give thanks if you feel sad at some point. When you win give thanks, and also give thanks when you lose.

Speak well about your friends, but also about people who do not speak well about you. You must speak well about all people and not gossip about anyone. If you feel you're going to criticize anyone, do not do it, when you want to give a compliment to someone, do it with the greatest enthusiasm.

"Love your neighbor as yourself. There is no commandment greater than these". - Mark 12:29-31

Love the rich, love the poor, love the youth, love the old, love the beauty and loves what is not so beautiful.

Everything around you was created by God, the God that is within you.

The rich do not want you to be poor, they know that this world is full of riches and, there is wealth for everyone. If they believed that there is no wealth for all, if they were envious of the happiness of others, they would not be rich and happy. Only unhappy people envy the happiness of others.

Take care of all that enters into your body, keep your body clean and be moderate, do not intoxique it with toxic food and garbage. Also watch what enters your mind, do not watch garbage TV programs, do not listen to those who are continually complaining because that is spread, and read good books, books to develop your soul and intelligence.

Remove from your vocabulary words like loss, abandonment, unable, impossible, improbable, failure, unworkable, hopeless and give up. Never be afraid, never hesitate, never despair, and THINK with an unbreakable FAITH that what you want is coming.

If you live in Africa or your origin is African, remember that Africa is full of riches. Africa has oil, diamonds, many different minerals, tropical woods, large reserves of water, abundant fish, wild animals and other countless riches, and the list is interminable.

But what´s the reason that many black men and women around the world and many Africans feel poor?

It is all in their way of THINKING, they have a poor mindset developed over hundreds of years, and that´s the only reason.

Europeans do not have any of these resources, but they have a wealth mentality developed over hundreds of years.

The only truth is that you are what you THINK about; to be rich, happy, smart, and intelligent, or anything else, you only have to think that you already are, no matter what others say, and no matter what happens around you.

Always keeping a positive thought about you may be hard and difficult, and that's the only reason that few people get to be truly rich.

People who achieve their goals have an unbreakable FAITH, and totally trust themselves and the God that is within them.

If you're surrounded by disease but you want health, think you're healthy. If you're surrounded by poverty but you want to be rich, think you're already rich.

The media gives a poor image about Africa and the Black men and women, just to keep them poor, but Africa is full of wealth.

When you are poor or sick, thinking about being rich or healthy could be difficult, but if you succeed, you will be the master of your fate, the captain of your soul. You'll get everything you want and be whoever you want to be.

Your only enemies are doubts and fear.

Wish to be around beautiful things, eat and drink moderately, cheer and brighten with your loved ones, travel, feed your mind, share and help your world, and God, who is within you, will help you if you believe and have FAITH.

In order to become or have anything you want, it is not necessary to fight with others, just create your own wealth. Neither take anything away from anyone or cheat, nor do illegal business.

There is nothing that anyone has, that you cannot have or be.

There may be some men and women who have achieved wealth attacking someone or with unpleasant business, but they have never been happy, they have lacked health or have never had someone who really loved them.

If you attack or steal, it is because you believe that there is not enough for everyone and, that is a poor mentality.

If you want something, you only have to IMAGINE yourself enjoying it in your thoughts, IMAGINE yourself having or being what you want to be or have, and keep an unbreakable FAITH about receiving it.

Do not talks about your deepest desires; keep them in your heart. Things around you will begin to change for you to receive what you want. Do not doubt.

"Do not be afraid, little flock, for your Father has been pleased to give you the kingdom". - Luke 12:32

God that is within you gives you everything you ask for, so be always grateful for what you have and are, grateful for your hands, your legs, for your brain, your hut or your mansion.

Be GRATEFUL for breathe and to be alive, everything that you have and are now is because you have thought about it, and God that is within you gave it to you.

If you want to change your world, you only have to change what you THINK about yourself and, be continually THANKFUL for what you have and what you are getting.

The more grateful you are with God that is within you, the more good things you will receive.

The richer and happier a person is, the more wealth and happiness he or she will receive. Many poor and unhappy people are not grateful, they only think about their poverty and unhappiness.

"Whoever has will be given more, and they will have an abundance. Whoever does not have, even what they have will be taken from them". - Matthew 13:12

To switch from rags to riches, or unhappiness to happiness, you only have to change your MINDSET.

THINK about wealth and happiness, think that you are receiving what you want and be continually thankful to God that is within you.

"Father, I thank You that You heard Me. I know that You always hear Me…". - John 1:1:41-42

Your father, who is God and is within you, gives you what you THINK you are, and THINK you have.

If you are always GRATEFUL and you THINK about the best, you will attract the best.

If you are THANKFUL and you have FAITH to wait for good things, good things will come.

It is very important to know what you want and desire it strongly. You have to keep in your mind a clear picture of what you want, and the type of person you want to become.

IMAGINE that you live with what you want to be and have, and wait it with FAITH and happiness.

"If you believe, you will receive whatever you ask in prayer".
- Matthew 21:22.

Praying is not going to Church and plead, praying is to THINK that you have what you want, and feel that you're already enjoying it, keep FAITH in your mind.

Let it be in your mind; living in your new home, feel you have fancy clothes, drive your new car, plan your trips and feel from inside that you are already enjoying all, it is very important that you feel it within you, because God, who is inside you is listening.

The use of your WILL is also very necessary to get what you want; you should not use your WILL against anyone or anything, only towards you.

Once you know what you want, ask for it and use your WILL to think and do the right things.

"Truly I tell you that if two of you on earth agree about anything they ask for, it will be done for them by my Father". - Matthew 18: 18-20.

The two people who have to agree are you and the God that is within you.

The WILL shall help to keep in your mind the vision of what you want, and to keep your FAITH in a continuous and stable way in that you're getting what you want, and be continually GRATEFULL.

Gradually you will realize that everything is changing so that you get what you want, all the things and people you will need in your life will appear.

Only the doubt, worry and fear are your enemies. THINK of the image you want with FAITH, and you will receive it.

The Bible says a lot about FAITH, you must have FAITH in God that is within you and gives you what you THINK you are, so **be careful about what you THINK you are.**

If you have been or are poor, do not talk about that, if you have been sick or someone is sick, do not talk about disease. If you've experienced hardship or someone around you have lived pain, forget about it.

"Let the dead bury their own dead" - Luke 9:60

If you want to help yourself and the people around you, THINK about becoming rich and happier, show them that it is easy to get what you THINK, and to get what you want.

You only have to keep a mental image of what you want and, THINK with an unbreakable FAITH that you're already getting it, that´s the secret.

If you start acting and THINKING as I say, everything around you will began to change, your government, the foreign governments, your family, the industry and even you will even begin to change.

Nothing can stop you if you THINK with FAITH in what you want, while you are GRATEFUL every day to the God that is within you.

"I and the Father are one."" - *John 10:30*

The Father is God who is within all men.

Before getting out of bed in morning, and before going to sleep at night, create a mental image of what you want or about who you want to be.

IMAGINE yourself enjoying that thing or having the qualities you want to have, keep this image with a happy feeling, THINKING that you have already achieved it, and be GRATEFULL to God that is within you for giving it to you.

Have FAITH and never doubt. That's the prayer.

"But when you pray, go away by yourself, shut the door behind you, and pray to your Father in private. Then your Father, who sees everything, will reward you". - Matthew 6: 6

Chapter 4. Love to find happiness.

Feeling love and giving love are the only ways of finding happiness in your life, there are also the best tools and essentials to create real wealth; the opposite of love is fear, doubt and insecurity.

If you feel love, all the negative disappears. If you feel love you will be able to bring happiness, joy and succeed in everything you do.

Love is what makes you happy in this life, without love life has little value and no sense. When you love, everything is easier and you no longer worry about race, social class or age.

When you love, you connect more easily with the God that is within you and the people and things you need to achieve your goals appear in your life.

But the negative publicity towards the African, the Western media and education was designed to belittle the non white, the memory of slavery and other things...have made the Black men and women accumulate insecurities and negative prejudices for hundreds of years.

Many black men and black women do not love themselves, but they have to understand that they only way to give true love and to receive true love are when you love yourself and those like you. There is no other way to happiness and true riches.

If someone has hurt you, forgive him, I am not saying that your relationship with this person has to be the same again, only forget the damage that is supposed someone done to you. It is important that you do, but not for the other, but for you.

If you forgive, you will feel better and happier; your life will change and shine. Resentment, hatred and evil thoughts make you unhappy, and that will not let you move.

"Forgive us our debts (offenses, sins) as we also have forgiven our debtors (those who have offended us or hurt)". - Matthew 6:12

To love yourself is to accept yourself as you are, God is deep within you and made you as you are, perfect.

When you love yourself, you love God and your life will be filled with happiness and wealth. Love yourself and you will have better health, you will have better relationships, you will be more creative and attract others to love you.

If you plant in your mind thoughts of love, happiness and wealth, you will attract love, happiness and wealth into your life.

If now you do not have the love of your life, do not push or pressure for him or her to appear, if he or she has not appeared yet, it may be because you are still not ready, or maybe the other person is not ready, in any case do not force things, everything has its time.

When you need some guidance lie down in the dark in a quiet place and relax, listen to your inner God, he will guide you if you're honest and true to yourself.

By the time you find your loved one, do not be afraid to give, if you are able to give, you will receive all from the other person.

In bed, if you want to receive pleasure, you must give pleasure. If you start to give more pleasure than the other person, he or she will be encouraged to do the same.

It is very important that your goal is not just to have an orgasm, but give all possible pleasure to your partner.

Chapter 5. Change what you think about yourself.

THINK for yourself, do not think what the media says you should think. Do not think what you were taught to think, erase and delete all the negative information they taught you about yourself.

Develop your character to THINK the best about yourself and not be influenced by anyone.

With your WILL and your new character, you will change everything around you, and you will achieve your goals.

No one can THINK for you, you create each day of your life with what you do and THINK. Control what you think and don´t be influenced by information from the past, tradition, television or magazines.

You have to understand that Western television is made for Westerners, if you identify with white people or white famous, you may have a disease.

To improve your character, you will have to act to yourself only, do not try to change others, and also don´t try to change the world. Others and situations will change for the better if you change for the better, do not criticize others and do not criticize yourself, just grow better every day.

What you can do to improve or discipline your character and will is; not listen to unpleasant things or anything you feel will not bring you any good; be brave to do and say the right thing at all times; do not be put off by appearances, hypocrisy or falsity; be persistent and do not give up.

IMAGINE with FAITH that what you want is coming, and give thanks for everything good happens to you, however small; keep your mind clear, drink and eat with moderation; forget about the problems of the past, if something or someone has insulted you or abandoned you, forget it.

Many times, when we have problems we focus on them and THINK too much about them, that's a mistake. You must THINK about the solution and the problem will disappear.

Pretend to be like Daniel who was in the lion's den but they did not do any harm to him, Daniel thought of God (the solution), if he had thought about the lions (the problems), they would have eaten him.

In every problem there is a bigger solution hidden, if you find the solution, you will be more intelligent, stronger, braver, more capable and have more confidence in yourself.

Once you control your THINKING and do not intoxicate yourself mentally or physically, you will see that everything will start changing. You will realize that it is as easy to be rich and happy, as to be poor and unhappy.

If you plant seeds of happiness, wealth, love, health and intelligence in your mind and do not have any doubt, if you keep your FAITH in that you are receiving what you want, you will receive the fruits.

Now you're laying the first stone of your future, the foundation of your wealth and happiness, you only have to have some patience.

"I am going to lay a rock in Zion, a rock that has been tested, a precious cornerstone, a solid foundation. Whoever believes will not worry." - Isaiah 28:16

If you hurry, feel fear, doubt or anxiety, you may kill the seeds you have already planted, if you think on the negative, you will attract it as easily, do not blame anyone for what happens to you any more, you are the only one responsible for what happens to you.

"No one can come to me unless the Father who sent me draws him" - John 6:44

Forget about past failures, if you THINK someone is above you, you're wrong. God, who is within you, did not make any person better than another.

Just keep an unbreakable FAITH that you are getting what you want.

In your life you may have great difficulties, you may believe that you are small or insignificant, many walls may stand up to you, but it's all in your mind. If you THINK you are capable, attractive, sexy, intelligent, free, strong and courageous, if you really THINK so, others will believe so.

"And there we saw the giants and we were in our own sight as grasshoppers, and so we were in their sight". - Numbers 13:33

You're a giant, the small and defenseless grasshoppers are your problems, and you can step them easily.

If you ever need some guidance, relax in a quiet dark room for few minutes and see how you will get some guidance.

Do not worry about how you will reach your goal; only THINK about your goal with happiness, and the persons or things you need, will appear in your life.

If you worry too much it is because you have doubts. Doubt and fear are your enemies.

When the means to reach your goal comes, you have to act with calm and joy, because inside you, you already know that you were going to achieve happiness and wealth.

If by the time you do not see clearly what to do, just continue with your normal business day, with peace and security.

"The ways of his providence are often unknown to us". - Corinthians 13:12

One of the aims of this book is to make you change what you THINK about yourself, if you read this book several times, you will see how little by little and day by day, you will be changing the negative beliefs ingrained in you since childhood.

You will distinguish the truth from the false, and you will only work on things that will help you be happier and richer.

Do not give up, do not ever fall into bad habits and, use your WILL to develop your self-control, get away from the "pleasures" of the moment and wait for the greater good.

You may have not previously realized about all the many negative things you did or said, maybe you were living in pain, fear and distress. Do not worry, forget about gossip, mocking laughter and lies, just forget the past.

"None of the offenses they have committed will be remembered." - Ezekiel 18:22

Do not ever remember the yesterday´s bad memories. Do not conserve your bad thoughts, do not be like Lot's wife who looked back and was preserved in salt.

THINK with FAITH that you're getting what you want; nobody is a victim of fate, but only a victim of little FAITH.

Now, your ACTIONS and your THOUGHTS are controlled by yourself, so THINK about happiness, wealth, love, freedom, health and intelligence.

"As a man thinketh in his heart, so is he and his life" - James Allen

Chapter 6. Final points for "afro people"

We are living in the best times for black men and women around the world; a great future is waiting for them, especially for the ones living in Africa.

Africa is returning to do things by itself and for itself, of which depends on its future. There has not been a better times than now for the past hundreds of years.

One of the reasons why I wrote this book is for us to become more aware of what is happening and has happened, for not to despise other African ethnic groups, and to be proud of our origins.

Ignorance is the only reason why many black men and women do not respected themselves, and more African knowledge will contribute to the progress of Africa and African descent worldwide.

Africa has a great artistic heritage; its art is rich and creative. The African who have studied their own art will realize that there are many differences between a Dogón mask, a Dan mask, guro, baga, etc., and that there is more imagination in the African art than in 25 centuries of Western sculpture.

Michelangelo and Rodin focused on muscular anatomy, discovered in Greece, forgotten by the Romans but rediscovered it in the Gothic art. It was redeveloped in the Renaissance, and re exploited in the academic art.

Yet in Africa, we must redevelop our art and our great music, full of sensitivity and rhythm. We must help our artists to enable them to express themselves as easily as Western artists.

We must learn to respect each other, help each other like other cultures do, the most important ally of Africans and black men and women are ourselves. Learn your history.

Slave trafficking and Western education was the worst things that happened to us, the Slave trafficking cannot be changed, but the education can be changed and re-written.

I am only trying to say that black men and women from Africa and around the world have a culture, race and common history, and we should support each other. We all need to be more responsible and aware of making things better with our effort.

About the author.

My name is Victor A. Nsue., I was born in Bata (Equatorial Guinea) in 1977, my mother was from Equatorial Guinea and, my father is from the Spanish Pyrenees.

I am not famous, nor Doctor, only someone with African origins who realized that Africa has a great history, beyond slavery. Someone who wants to forget about cultural divisions and, improve the economic security of men and women with African origins. And also discover some hidden truths.

There have been and exist black scientists, black revolutionaries, black sovereigns, black philosophers, black artists and writers.

With the help of readers, I hope to continue writing and translating books that improve the knowledge of our past to become more aware of whom we are and have been.

Victor A. Nsue
victornsue@gmail.com

About the Book Cover Artists

Pau Mar (Paulina Márquez) is a Cuban artist. His works are symbolic representations of the essence of the Cuban woman; spiritual guide and the protective mother that our African ancestors left us.

The need to deepen and explore in the study of the African legacy is one of the reasons in her work. In her work we find elements of Africa referred to in allegorical form, and works related to gender and races are recurrent.

About Book Cover

"Corazón del monte"

It is a tribute to our ancestors and wants to give voice to the millions of people who died as a result of greed, disease and the inhumane treatment of slave traffic.

It tells us about that identity that comes to us from the times of slavery. It tells us of the pain of migrations and sorrows, but also of the wonder that all is not lost.

That´s right, all is not lost. We have bodies and rituals. We have art, we have the wings to take the flight, to continue the story by correcting the capital omissions, and reign the earth with the permission of our ancestors.

Back cover:

This book is not a theory book; the focus is entirely practical and goes to the root of why many black men and women or descendants of Africans fail to find happiness and wealth. The text is straightforward and clear, if the reader memorizes it, he or she will not have the need to go and look for similar books.

In the book you will find the most important information after reading dozens of books about African and European classical philosophy, spirituality, history, personal development, economics and finance. All this combined with my own life experience.

The book has few pages, but I would have summarized all down to one sentence:

"In life, we are what we think most of the day"

But what are you thinking about? Are you aware of your thoughts? Why are you thinking what you think?

We all know that many negative messages have been sent against black men and women for hundreds of years, and these negative publicity have sank their self-esteem and security, also this negative publicity is still working today throughout the world to maintain us asleep and unable.

But the solution to this is simple and, in this book I have tried to explain it.

Hope this will help.

www.ingramcontent.com/pod-product-compliance
Lightning Source LLC
Chambersburg PA
CBHW031434250726
48656CB00002B/975